UNCOMPROMISING

Love

LYNETTE EDWARDS

Trafford rev. 01/25/2013

 www.trafford.com

North America & international
toll-free: 1 888 232 4444 (USA & Canada)
phone: 250 383 6864 ♦ fax: 812 355 4082

CONTENTS

ACKNOWLEDGEMENTS

To the love of my soul, my comforter, true provider, and source of my strength, Jesus Christ; there is no way I would be alive without grace and mercy.

To my parents, I wouldn't change you for the world. I love you both just as you are and I am proud that God chose you to be part of my life.

My sisters/best friends Precious Boudreaux and Kayla Minix; I am proud of the women you are. Keep pressing toward the mark and you shall receive your crown.

Kennedi and Kendall Boudreaux, my heart melts when I think of your innocence and kind hearts. I pray that God will send angels to encamp around you so that you are able to walk in the path of righteousness.

Latonia Riggs, Brandy Leday, Rhonda Watson, Linton Edwards Jr., Brandon Gallow, and Phillip Gallow Jr., we grew up as siblings, I hope and pray that you never give up on God because he will never give up on you.

Derrell Boudreaux, Christopher Minix, and Murphy Riggs you have an important role to play in the lives of your family; as long as you place God at the head of your life you will be able to effectively be the head of your house.

To my Pastor, Lloyd Joiner Jr. and the Progressive Baptist Church family, thank you for allowing me to use the gifts that God has given me within the walls of the church. My prayer is that God will allow Progressive to continue to grow on the word of God and do great and marvelous works for years to come.

To those that went before me: Linton Edwards Sr., Idelia Edwards, Louanna Jack, Wilson Jack Sr., Ronald Jack, Etna Mae Jack, David Jack, Crystal Jack, Amelia Leday, and Debra Hebert; may you rest in the arms of our loving savior and spend an eternity in peace.

UNCOMPROMISING LOVE

Betrayed, hurt, and in agony, yet choosing to endure so that someone else can live for an eternity; that's love.

Walking the earth for three years though persecuted for living a pleasing life, yet never giving up on the mission; that's love.

Forsaking friends and loved ones and giving up your own desires for a perfect stranger though you may never hear the words 'thank you'; that's love.

Getting beat for hours yet refusing to compromise, then hanging on a cross with criminals though you never committed a crime, enduring it all without mumbling a word; that's love.

When Jesus died he had you and I in mind; that's uncompromising love.

CHAPTER 1

THE ULTIMATE SACRIFICE

B eaten and bruised beyond recognition. Placed on a cross among criminals. Hands stretched wide. Head hung low. He never mumbled a word. He then took his last breath and died. I don't know about you but to me that sounds like the ultimate sacrifice.

Without the sacrifice on Calvary I dread to imagine where I would be.

When I think about how Jesus literally gave up what he could have been so that I can be what he wants me to be, it truly makes me appreciate the sacrifice on Calvary.

All too often we take the sacrifice in vein and though we understand what was done on our behalf we seemingly forget that without that sacrifice we wouldn't be alive today.

I have sacrificed many things in my life but to unselfishly die and end my life on earth just so that you can have life more abundantly. I must be honest and admit that there is no way that I can humbly do such a thing. Yet Jesus did it. He did it so that all of God's children can live a life pleasing to his father. Not a perfect life, but a life giving honor and glory to the almighty king.

I urge you not to allow the ultimate sacrifice to be in vein. I beg you to take a moment and rethink of all the times you purposely did wrong and how you selfishly gave in to the temptation of the world. Now for a moment think about Jesus, covered with blood, sweat, and tears then willingly hanging his head low and obediently accepting the will of the father.

My God, what a sacrifice, Jesus truly demonstrated uncompromising love.

What are you willing to sacrifice?

CHAPTER 2

YOU HAVE A CHOICE

B arnabas was a man who had committed multiple murders. A man who some would call crazy, others vindictive. Yet no one denied that he was in deed a murderer. Jesus committed no crimes. There was no sufficient evidence of any crime being committed, yet a crowd of his peers ordered that he be put to death. Someone could have ordered that Jesus be set free and that Barnabas be kept in chains for the crimes that he had committed yet no one said a word. A choice had to be made. It was clear that someone had to die. But who?

Everyday you and I are faced with countless of choices. What will I wear? Where will I shop? What shall I eat?

There are millions of daily choices yet eternity only has two; heaven or hell. I hope you chose wisely.

I often sit back and think about the choices I have made in my life thus far. Some were good while others were horrible yet I wouldn't change one choice. Why? I am so glad you asked. Sit back and relax while I explain. Everything in your life happens for a reason. Though you don't understand it now you must remember that nothing happens by chance, accident, or coincidence. God has purposely allowed you to be exactly where you are at this exact moment. It is when we realize that we can't change the past, and that the future is already taken care of that we are able to take heed to what is being done in the present. All you have is this moment. Can I tell you that you are as close to God right now as you will ever be. Why? Because God is omnipresent which means that he is everywhere at the same time.

I dare you to make the choice to be free. Choose to be happy. Choose to make decisions that will change your life for the better.

I get sick to my stomach when I sit back and think about how we purposely make the wrong choices. Don't let the death of Jesus be in vein. When he hung on the cross it was not because he personally was ready to leave the earth but instead it was because he knew that the work of his father had to be completed. Don't let that work be in vein. Jesus made the sacrifice to humbly die for you, now is the time that you willingly sacrifice for him. Choose this day whom you will serve.

CHAPTER 3

THE BLOOD STILL WORKS

I woke up in horrible pain. I could hardly swallow and it felt as though my throat was closing in on me. Not knowing what to do or who to call I began to cry because of all the pain I was in. I then found the strength to get to the telephone and call my sister. I asked her to quickly come and transport me to the emergency room. Once there I was immediately taken to be seen by a physician. He quickly gave me a shot to num the pain, then after about two hours of waiting to see how much of an effect the shot would have on me I was prescribed three bottles of pills to be administered daily until all of the pain was gone. The doctor informed me that my tonsils were severely infected and the infection had spread causing my glands to swell. According to the doctor the medicine would help but if this pain ever arose again I would have to have emergency surgery.

Approximately a year and a half later I woke up to a familiar pain. I could barely swallow and my tonsils were so infected that when I opened my mouth I could see the infection on my tonsils. When I touched my neck it would hurt due to my glands being swollen. It was as though I had awoken out of a bad dream. The same sickness that I experienced over a year prior was happening all over again. I began to cry because all I could remember was the words of the doctor replaying in my mind "Lynette you will have to have emergency surgery if this reoccurs". Those words made me terrified. All I could think about was that I did not want to be hospitalized and just as I was getting ready to pick up the telephone, as I did the last time, to call my sister I remembered that the doctor does not have the last word in my life.

I began to cry out to the Lord. I cried not because I was in pain, but I cried because I needed the Lord. I needed him to wrap his loving hands around me and reassure me that everything would be alright. I needed him to be a doctor in a sick room. I then touched my throat and began to pray. I prayed that God would heal me and take away all sickness from my body. I prayed until I literally could not pray anymore and after I prayed I laid down in my bed and went to sleep believing that God would heal me. I awoke and was still in pain so I decided to pray some more. I spent two days praying every chance I got and on the second day I was totally, not partially, but TOTALLY healed! There was no pain in my body, the infection had seized, and I felt better than ever. I am a living witness that the blood still works.

Can I tell you that man has limited power but God has all power? With the doctor and all his man made medicine it took two weeks for me to be healed but with Jesus after just one touch in his perfect timing all was well.

The blood never changes. Morning, noon, evening, and night from dawn to dusk the blood will still be the same.

CHAPTER 4

JESUS, JESUS, JESUS

One of the songs that I frequently remember my mom singing when I was a little girl was "Oh How I Love Jesus." I must be honest I was not raised in the church yet when I would hear that song the hairs on my arm would rise. I just loved any mention of the name of Jesus. That name sets my soul on fire, turns my darkness into days, and my sorrow into joy. The name Jesus is so powerful that demons tremble and mountains by faith will move. Jesus, Jesus, Jesus. How sweet is that name. I don't know how you feel about it but I love Jesus.

It is hard to love what/who you know nothing about. In other words if all you do is get on your knees and pray the

'Our Father' prayer than get off your knees and go to bed then you my friend may indeed be praying to an unknown God.

Now I know you know a few scriptures and it is good that you take communion monthly but do you know Jesus?

In case you don't know him let me take a few minutes to inform you about the man from Galilee. Born the son of a virgin and a carpenter, as a young boy could be found teaching in the temple, the only one who was able to take two fish and five loaves a bread and feed five thousand, biblical records of him fasting for forty days and forty nights, he went to hell and preached a revival, he allowed a blind man to see, a crippled man to walk, and a lame man to talk, healed a woman with a twelve year issue of blood, turned water into wine, humbly was beaten and bruised then humbly hung on a cross and took the abuse, he took it for you, he took it for me, he then hung his head down low, stretched his arms out wide, closed his eyes and freely gave himself away. He was buried in a borrowed tomb. Then on the third day he got up with all power, and he is still alive today.

Now that you know about him why don't you help me call his name: JESUS, JESUS, JESUS.

There comes a time in your life when you will have to know him for yourself. It's good that your mother knows Jesus; it's great that your daddy can call upon the name of Jesus. But if I can keep it real for a minute let me remind you that your mother can't stand up for you on judgment day and your daddy does not have the power to place you in heaven.

We are each accountable for only one person; ourselves. It doesn't matter who you start your race with, the fact of the matter is when you get to the finish line it's all about you. Who else makes it or who gives in is not your priority.

Let's get back to what matters the most. Let's get back to Jesus. He can walk with you and talk with you but you have to be willing to let him. Easy directions, yet very hard to follow if your mindset is not on Jesus.

How do you keep your mindset on Jesus? I am so glad you asked. You keep your mindset on Jesus by focusing not on earthly things but on that which is of Jesus. Where your treasure is, that is where your heart it.

If that brand new car is what gives you your greatest joy then that my friend is where your heart will be. If finances is what motivates you through your day than it may be difficult to think of anything else. You have to make the decision to focus on Jesus. And if I may say so myself making the decision to focus on Jesus will be the first of best decisions that you will ever make.

Once your mind is set on Jesus it is then that you as a person can become one with Jesus. My, what a time you will have when you are one with your savior. Nothing and no one comes close to the intimacy between a father and a child.

CHAPTER 5

DEATH DID NOT WIN

I can only imagine the celebration that took place when those that beat and tortured Jesus had when they learned of his death. They accused him of blasphemy and ordered that he be crucified. And just as they requested he was beaten, tortured, hung, and died. So I can just imagine how they must have partied and celebrated as they had crucified the one that they seemingly hated. They put him in his grave and they just knew that it was the end but little did they know that it was only the beginning.

Death did not win. On the third day Jesus got up. He got up because death could not over take him. He got up because there was so much more for him to do. He got up for you. He got up for me. He got up because death could not win.

A love one dies and it is human nature for us to mourn. The bible says that even Jesus wept. We are upset and it hurts to know that we can no longer call on that person. No more shopping or eating out with them. Death seems so final and indeed feels at times like it is an ending when the reality is that it is actually the beginning of an eternity with our father.

Death did not win with Jesus and in Jesus name it will not end with you. Inheriting eternal life if very simple, you accept Christ as your Lord and Savior and you too shall inherit your fathers' kingdom.

Now if that doesn't excite you I don't know what will. All I have to do is confess with my mouth and believe in my heart that Jesus has died for me and I am an heir of the throne. Lord have mercy.

How can something so seemingly easy be so hard; one word, Satan. That no good, evil, lying, good for nothing enemy roams the earth to make your life a living hell. Every time you take two steps forward, the enemy purposely pulls you three steps back. When you are down he pushes you even lower. His job is to keep you in the past and convince you that you have no future when the truth of the matter is that all he has is the past and can't find a future to save his soul.

Don't get pulled in the enemy's trap. Guard your weak areas with all that you have. The enemy will purposely prey on the areas in which you are weak.

Death did not win. The enemy is defeated and you my friend have the victory. You are more than a conqueror. Believe it and by faith you shall receive and inherit the kingdom of God.

CHAPTER 6

LOSE YOURSELF IN JESUS

Falling in love with someone is truly amazing. You meet that person and you spend hours getting to know one another. Laughing at all of the jokes and crying at the mention of a sad story. Day by day you take the time learning the person's ways and worries. You become in sync with whom they are and you learn ways to make them smile.

Before you know it you lose yourself in that person. You are able to do so because you now trust that person. You trust that they have your best interests at heart and you pray that they never let you down.

The same way that you are able to lose yourself in that man or woman you are in love with, you should be able to lose yourself in Jesus.

Losing yourself is easier said than done. When one loses themselves, they are no longer in control. They have allowed the one that they are giving themselves away to, to take total control. In order to lose control you must trust.

The bible tells us that we should lean not to our own understanding but in all of our ways acknowledge God. The words "in all our ways" means with everything we have.

For a minute right now, this minute I want you to lose yourself. Don't lose yourself in man but instead the one that made all man; lose youself in God. Forget about your significant other, children, job, family, friends, neighbors, enemies, doubt, and fears. Forget about what you did last night and what you were just thinking about doing later tonight. I want you to sit back, relax, and imagine your savior standing in front of you with arms stretched open unto you. Imagine the smile on his face as you get up and begin to embrace him. Imagine him wrapping his arms around you and gently whispering in your ear that he loves you and has been waiting on this very moment for you to decide to lose yourself in him. Wow. What a feeling. What an amazing spirit-filled time you will have in the arms of Jesus.

Lose yourself in him. Let him take control of your heart, mind, body, and soul. He has already sacrificed his entire life for you. He is now waiting on you to trust him with the life that he has given you so that he can show you what real love truly is. Lose yourself in Jesus; he wants you just as you.

CHAPTER 7

SALVATION IS FREE BUT IT IS NOT CHEAP

Nothing in this life is free with the exception of salvation. Anyone young, old, black, white, it does not matter you can be saved and it will not cost you one red cent. And the best news of all is that when you are saved once, you are saved for life. You don't have to read the prayer of salvation every Sunday nor do you have to get "resaved" every time you stray away from the will of God. In fact the bible tells us in the book of Romans that we all fall short. In other words you are not perfect. I am not perfect. And the fact of the matter is that neither of us will ever be perfect. But thankfully we all have the opportunity to choose salvation and serve a perfect God who uses imperfect people.

Even though salvation is free, it is far from being cheap. It will indeed cost you. It may cost you friends and family or pride and humility but it will cost you.

Once you are saved there is a sacrificial process that must occur. You have to crucify your flesh and allow your spirit to lead. Crucifying the flesh is hard because you wake up with the flesh; you work with the flesh, and go to bed with the flesh. But in order to successful live a life according to the will of God you have to make the decision to crucify your flesh daily.

I know you have your own agenda, so do I. But when it is all said and done, not now nor has it ever been about you or your petty pre-occupations. You have to die to self, which simply means you have to freely give yourself away to God.

How much does it cost to sacrifice? I can't put a monetary price on the cost but I can tell you that I have lost family members, friends, time away from doing what I loved, I have missed family functions and have had to cry more times than I can count, but I wouldn't change any of my sacrifices for anyone in this world.

The cost of sacrifice is costly but if you are truly sacrificing from your heart it will pay off in a way that is beyond your wildest expectations.

What exactly are you willing to sacrifice to get to where you want to be? Salvation is indeed free, but the cost of living a life pleasing to God may cost you more than you expected to pay.

CHAPTER 8

NOT GUILTY

Daniel was placed in the lions' den for refusing to only bow down to the king. He spent the night in a lions den yet the lions did not bite him. The next day the king went down to the den and found that the lions had not bitten Daniel, he then freed Daniel, he was not guilty of the wrong they earlier accused him of doing.

David was a small boy who went against a mighty giant by the name of goliath. Though goliath was notorious for winning fights across the land David fought him and won. There is not a jury in the world that would convict David; not guilty.

Jonah refused to go to the town of Nineveh as instructed by God and instead he made the decision to go to Tarnish and follow his own plans. God then purposely sent forth a storm in which Jonah was thrown in the sea. A big fish swallowed Jonah and he spent three days in the belly of the fish praying and then arrived safely in the town of Nineveh as planned by God, though Jonah was disobedient there is not enough evidence to built a strong case; not guilty.

You sinned on yesterday, willfully lied to your spouse, stole from your employer, and thought impure thoughts. You have broken more commandments this year alone then most people have throughout their lives. There are recordings of your wrong doings and lawyers are literally fighting at a chance to take your case and lock you up in prison for as long as the law allow. The state hires a lawyer to argue a case against you but knowing that you have no money to afford an attorney you go alone. Only when you get to the courthouse sure that you will lose because of the evidence laid out an advocate steps in on your behalf. He never studied at any accredited university nor has he completed the required amount of hours interning in the state, yet he has never lost a case. The judge walks in and sees all of the evidence against you presented by the state's attorney and is ready to lock you up but just at the nick of time your lawyer steps in and defends you. The judge makes his decision; not guilty.

When you allow Jesus into your life he defends you at any cost. He doesn't bring up past records of wrong doing.

In fact he casts all of your sins previously committed as far as the east is from the west. And since the east and west never meet there is never any mention of your sins. God is a lawyer who is undefeated. He has never once lost a case. That my friend is the type of lawyer we all need on our side.

Jesus and his people verses the world; NOT GUILTY.

CHAPTER 9

JUST ONE TOUCH FROM THE MASTER

Nobody and I do mean nobody can do me like Jesus. He is the love of my life, the light to my darkness and the reason there is a smile on my face. There is something about Jesus that puts him in a class all by himself. He is all that I am not yet everything that I long to be.

You may have been touched by man, and no doubt that it felt good.

But there is a touch that can't be measured by man's hand and a touch that doesn't compare to anything on earth. It is the touch from the master. A light gentle touch that has the power to ease troubled minds and heal broken hearts. There is something about his touch that makes all well with his children.

There was a woman in the bible that had an issue of blood. She had been bleeding for twelve years and could not seem to be cured. This woman was a woman of faith. For she knew that if she could just touch the hem of Jesus' garments, she would be made whole. She knew that Jesus had the touch that could do the seemingly impossible. She knew that if she just had faith she would be healed by the power of Jesus.

According to the bible after the woman with the issue of blood touched Jesus' garment she was healed. It had nothing to do with the life she lived or any special education she possessed, yet it had everything to do with her belief in Jesus and the power of that of her heavenly father.

If you have never experienced the masters touch now is a good time to open your heart. You have to understand that it wasn't that the woman asked to be healed and it was so. It was because she sought God with her heart. God knows the heart of all of his children. When you open your heart to God he is able to work on you from the inside out. And then as a result what is on the inside moves on the outside and others are able to see who you are.

I want a touch from the master; in fact I yearn for his touch daily. His touch will allow you to soar higher than any eagle and fly to new heights in him. You and I both need the touch of a master and lucky for us his touch is just as powerful today as it was over a thousand years ago.

He is waiting for you to reach out to him with your heart; the question is how bad do you want it?

CHAPTER 10

STANDING IN THE NEED OF PRAYERS

It is not my brother nor is it my sister but it's me standing in the need of prayer.

There is truly power in prayer. It doesn't matter what the situation may be when you are in the need of prayer and you firmly stand on the word of God, heaven opens up and tunes in to what you have to say.

I don't know about you but I am desperately in need of prayer. The bible says that the closer we get to God the closer that he will draw to you. In other words when I stand in the need of prayer and I am bold enough to call out his name God then comes close to me. And the closer I call the closer he draws near.

Life sometimes gets hard. We have to cry and fight and fight and cry day after day. That is why it is essential that God's people stand firmly and pray. I am not speaking of the pattern 'Our Father' prayer, but I am speaking of prayer from your heart.

You may not pray like the deacons or be as deep as the pastor but when you pray from your heart you are seeking God diligently and that is what he wants. He wants your all. Not just a pattern prayer that you say out of tradition or a moment of silence. He wants everything that has breath to praise him and he truly deserves it.

It is time that you stand and begin to pray for yourself. Don't call on someone else to do what God has equipped you to do for yourself. You have the power because you have God on the inside that can move on the outside and make his presence known in your life.

Someone once said that there is a certain way that you must go to God. The person tried explaining to me exactly what I must say and what order I should recite certain words when I pray. I must be honest because I never prayed the way the person instructed me to pray. Instead I decided to open up my mouth and speak from my heart. And every time I do I can feel the presence of God.

Now don't get me wrong I strongly believe in reverencing God and taking time to pray but when you are truly under the covering of God it is not what pattern in which you pray but it is the words that you pray from your heart and soul.

The next time that you are standing in the need of prayers I want you to open your mouth and be real with God. Take off the mask and unveil who you are. Give him your heart and believe that he sees all, knows all, and hears all.

There is power in prayer that comes from your heart.

CHAPTER 11

IT IS NOT ABOUT YOU

The flesh must be crucified daily. There are no if, ands, or buts about it. You must crucify your flesh. The bible says in Matthew 26:41 that we must watch and pray so that we do not fall into temptation because the spirit is willing but the flesh is weak. In other words your spirit wants to do well, it wants to walk right and live right but the flesh wants the exact opposite.

You must crucify your flesh (which is not always simple to do) because you wake up with the flesh, you work with the flesh; you go to bed with the flesh.

The truth is that you can not be spirit fed until you are spirit led. You can't be spirit led until you feed the spirit. Just like the outer man needs bread to eat, you need spiritual food. Lucky for you there are sixty-six books from Genesis to Revelation that can feed your spirit. Why don't you take and minute a try Genesis, Exodus, Leviticus, Numbers, Deuteronomy, Joshua, Judges, Ruth, 1 Samuel, 11 Samuel, 1 Kings, 11 Kings, 1 Chronicles, 11 Chronicles, Ezra, Nehemiah, Esther, Job, Psalms, Proverbs, Ecclesiastes, Song of Songs, Isaiah, Jeremiah, Lamentations, Ezekiel, Daniel, Hosea, Joel, Amos, Obadiah, Jonah, Micah, Nahum, Habakkuk, Zephaniah, Haggai, Zechariah, Malachi, Matthew, Mark, Luke, John, Acts, Romans, 1Corinthians, 11 Corinthians, Galatians, Ephesians, Philippians, Colossians, 1 Thessalonians, 11 Thessalonians, 1 Timothy, 11 Timothy, Titus, Philemon, Hebrews, James, 1 Peter, 11 Peter, 1 John, 11 John, 111 John, Jude, and Revelation. Sixty six books with countless verses guaranteed to lead you to the path of righteousness.

I know you would love to think that it's about you and that you had something to do with where you are in your life and as much as I hate to burst your bubble I must be clear when I remind you that God was in control before you were born unto this earth and he will remain in control after your soul is ascended from this earth unto your heavenly home.

God is in control of your yesterday, today, and has thankfully already taken care of your tomorrow.

It takes time to humble yourself in a way that you are able submit yourself to God. When you submit yourself to

God you are able to allow him to lead in a way that you are able to see who he is and what he does in your life. It is when you see all of the wonders he does that you are able to see that it is indeed all about him.

He is a God who wants you to love yourself in a way that you are able to deny yourself but not forget who you are in Christ.

CHAPTER 12

HE IS GOD ALONE

I can't say how many times I have stated: "God is taking too long to answer my prayers so let me step in and assist him" Typical statement yet one that will hinder a prayer rather than hurry it. The truth of the matter is that you can't hurry God and he surely doesn't need your help. Just so that we are clear let me clarify by saying that God didn't need your help last night when he put you to sleep and he doesn't need your help today when he strengthens you through your journey. He is God all by himself.

We must all understand that God's timing and our timing may not be the same. In fact it is often very different.

God does not move when we tell him to move. You can't manipulate him nor is there some magic potion that you can take that will make God move. God moves when it is his ordained time.

Faith and patience is the key that unlocks the door to trust. Faith is believing that Jesus will come through. But it takes more than faith; it takes patience. We all must be able to wait on the Lord. Though he is faithful, we as his children are not. We have to learn how to stand on his word at all times.

The awesome thing about God is that he does not need your help. In other words put your hand in the hand of the man who is able to do all things but fail.

Putting your life in the hand of God is easier said than done. In fact I don't mind putting my life in his hands, the problem is that when I become impatient I take my life out of his hands and I take control of the situation.

But on my own I have come to the understanding that I need to let go and let God handle every situation that I encounter. You and I both need to understand that just like the chair that you sit in is made to keep you from falling, so is the Lord. He can handle every situation both big and small.

He is God all by himself. He was here before you stepped foot on this earth and he will be here after you leave.

Faith and patience unlocks the key to trusting God. Once you have unlocked the key, you will have access to all that you need to allow God to order your steps in the will of the Lord.

I know it's hard, but be still because God does not need your help.

CHAPTER 13

TRUE LOVE

He awakes me every morning and puts me back to sleep at night. When I am lonely he comforts me, when I am tired he gives me the strength I need to make it one more day. When I am confused he regulates my mind. He is better than slice bread sweeter than sweet potato pie. He walks with me and talks with me and reassures me that I am his. He allows me to fall in love with him over and over and over and over again. He then leads me to a place where only he and I share, a place that man doesn't understand and the world will never be able to comprehend. He doesn't put me down or speak negatively to me. Instead he shows me that my tomorrows will be better that my today and he cast my past out of my thoughts by reminding me of the promises that I will soon receive. His love for me is real and he promised to remain true until the end of time. He sacrificed who he could have been so that I can be all that he wants me to be.

True love is what Jesus has for each and every one of his loving children. True love is walking the earth for three years and then dying an unselfish death all for someone that is not worthy.

True love was demonstrated when Jesus hung his head low and stretched his arms wide on that old rugged cross.

Until you have felt the true love of Jesus, you will never truly understand what true love is. We often settle in relationships because we feel as though we have found love. The love that we "found" starts off amazing but at often times it ends without a moments notice. Then we wander looking and searching for love only to discover that what we want is what we already have.

Once you fall in love with your savior you will experience real love. Don't just take my word for it; fall in love for yourself.

True love is patient, kind, everlasting, not boastful, and not envious. True love is a love that remains true until the very end.

Falling in love with Jesus was the best thing that I have ever done.

CHAPTER 14

EVERYTHING IN ITS' APPOINTED TIME

I have spent countless of hours fasting and praying for God to miraculously send all that he promised me. I still can't quite understand why I am still awaiting visions to come. Everything that was prayed on yesterday could have been given to me the second I asked but instead I am still waiting.

Though it gets rough and I become impatient on a daily basis I know that everything will happen in God's appointed timing. The fact of the matter is that I can fast and pray until I am black and blue in the face but I will not get what God has for me until he sees fit. It will all happen in his appointed timing.

The bible tells us that there are seasons for everything. You wouldn't fly a kite in the winter time nor would you wear a fur coat in the summer. There is a season for all things and in its' season all is well.

When you receive what you want outside the time that it is appointed for it doesn't happen in the matter that God predestined.

I know you feel as though it is your time but I urge you to be patient. The bible says to be still and know that he is God. Since he is God he knows when the time is right for you to receive your blessings. Let me say it one more time in case you missed it. GOD'S TIMING IS THE BEST TIME.

His plan is never to make you wait for you to get bitter but instead he wants you to become better. He wants each and every one of his children to look up to him and trust that he has everything under control.

God has your best intentions at heart and he wants nothing more than to bless his children.

Keep believing, keep praying, and keep waiting. If God said it, it shall surely come to pass in his appointed timing.

CHAPTER 15

SPEAK LIFE INTO YOUR CURRENT SITUATION

L ife and death is in the power of the tongue. Though the tongue has no organs it is able to kill self esteem within two seconds of speaking negatively to someone.

The widow woman in the Old Testament in the bible only had a few empty jars yet owed a great debt. She didn't curse herself but instead she sought help. She was then obedient and filled the jars as instructed and the bible says that not only were the widow's debt paid off but she had enough of what she needed for an additional seven years.

We must learn how to speak life into our situations. If you are sick speak a healing, if you are discouraged speak encouragement; if you are lonely speak comfort; if you are in need of finances speak prosperity.

You have more power than you realize. You are the head and not the tail. You must make a conscious decision to live and not die.

Though you are alive in the flesh you may be dead in the spirit.

It is time for you to feed your spirit so that you may live. Speak it and believe it. The bible says that if you have faith as small as a mustard seed you can move mountains. The mustard seed is the smallest seed in the garden yet it grows to be the biggest seed in the garden.

With faith those dead situation must seize. You have the power but it is up to you to use it.

Call those things that are not as though they are. God is waiting for you just where you are.

Stand up and speak life, for this is a day that the Lord has made be glad and rejoice in it.

CHAPTER 16

LIVING IN THE OVERFLOW OF BLESSINGS

I am blessed in the city. I am blessed in the field. I am blessed going in and I am even blessed coming out. I am living in the overflow not because of my education or family background. I am living in the overflow because of my heavenly father.

We as the seeds of Abraham have to remember that our father owns everything. We need to come out of the mindset that we can only have what our paycheck allows. Now in no means am I suggesting that you act foolishly and spend what you do not posses, but I do suggest that you seek God for what he has to give you.

The bible says in the book of Philippians that God will supply all of our needs according to his riches. In other words, he will give you what he feels you are in need of according to his will.

When I speak of the overflow of blessing I don't refer to only money and riches of that nature, but I refer to the peace of mind, wisdom, sound understanding, and the amazing fruits of the spirit of the Lord (patience, gentleness, kindness, love, joy, peace, meekness, self-control, and goodness).

It is time that we tap into the spiritual blessings that were promised to us before we were even conceived. It is time to live in the overflow of blessings. No offense to you but I refuse to die before I receive heaven; I want to taste heaven here on God's beautiful green earth.

I want the peace that surpasses all human understanding, the joy that the world can't give me nor can they ever take away. I want to wake up worshiping instead of worrying and I want that healing touch felt from my father every morning.

It is time that we tap into what is owed to us. You wouldn't work a forty hour week without getting paid would you? I didn't think so, therefore just as you expect a paycheck on Friday afternoon you should expect to receive the promises from the Lord daily.

It is time to come out of darkness, come out of sickness, come out of pain and walk into the overflow of blessings.

It is here if you want it. All it takes is you seeking your true provider.

CHAPTER 17

DO NOT COMPROMISE

M oney is tight so instead of waiting for God to supply we run to the local pay day loan and borrow money to get by. The only problem is that next month I have to not only pay the money I borrowed back but on top of that I have interest to pay, all because of compromising.

Money was tight with me at one point in my life and it didn't seem to ever get better. I met this guy and in less than a month of knowing him he invited me to move in with him. I was not physically attracted to him nor was there anything from him that I wanted other than a friendship but the fact of the matter was that if I moved in with him

I would be free financially and I would have time to save money. Of course I thought about it for at least a week and as much as I needed a way out of my bills God would not let me compromise.

Let me be clear when I say that God would not let me compromise. I personally was going to compromise. I thought if I did it for a little while it would help me in the end, but thank God he is in control. He just wouldn't let it be. His hand of protection was so wrapped around me that I couldn't move in with this man to save my life. God blocked it.

We all must learn not to compromise. It gets hard but God shall supply all of our needs according to his riches. We have to believe that and stand on those words when life gets rough.

Compromising is not of God. You can't choose to do right today than purposely sin on tomorrow. God will make a way if you just wait. On of my favorite bible verses is Psalm 46:10 because part of that verse says to be still and know that he is God. Be still means do not move, know that he is God means he will move you if he wants to.

I know it's rough, but be still. I know you are tired, but be still. I know your day seems dark and bleak, but be still. God has not forgotten about you. He will come through but you have to believe.

Be still and know that he is God.

CHAPTER 18

UNFAILING LOVE

Piercing his side at every turn, I refused to go into the church and pray, refused to be obedient. I simply had enough.

Prayers were not answered in a timely manner and I wasn't getting any younger; enough was enough. I refused to walk this so called Christian life any longer.

For weeks I tried on my own to make it outside the will of God. I knew that I was smart enough to live a life that was pleasing to me; or so I thought.

Through all the many times of refusing to obey and purposely do my own agenda, God's love remained the same; unfailing.

Not once did he count me out. Instead each time he opened his arms to me with grace and mercy reassuring me that he would protect me and give me the desires of my heart.

Unfailing love is a type of love that doesn't thin out when things get thick. It doesn't come on Monday and leave on Friday.

Unfailing love is a love that is around twenty four hours a day three hundred sixty four days out of the year.

Unfailing love is what Jesus shows us each and every day.

Fall in love with Jesus and allow him to show you what real love is. Allow him to gently take your hand and walk you through this life.

He will show you a love like no other. He will keep you and protect you from all hurt and danger. He will be your best friend when you are friendless.

God will show you a love like no other. I know you may feel as though you have slipped out of the grace of God but the truth of the matter is that at this very moment you are exactly where God wants you to be.

You are in the perfect place to release yourself to the Lord. He is waiting for you with arms stretched out wide. He is standing in front of your with unfailing love ready to share with you the blessings that await you.

CHAPTER 19

GRACE AND MERCY

It is God's grace that carries me and God's mercy that will keep me. Why he loves me I will never know, but one thing I do know is that his grace and mercy keeps me even though I don't deserve it. Grace can't be measured on a weighing scale. It isn't something we can save all our money to receive. Grace is what we receive from our father just because he loves us.

I often think about the stories in the Old Testament in the bible and my heart breaks because of how strict some of the laws of the land were but then I begin to read books in the New Testament and I get excited. You see it was that ultimate sacrifice on Calvary that allowed you and me to still be here today.

Without grace I would have died in one of the many car accidents I had, drowned in the pool I once tried swimming in, and possibly even committed suicide when I was down and out. I don't know about you but I thank God for his grace and mercy. I can't live without grace and mercy and neither can you

CHAPTER 20

BE OBEDIENT

Don't look back; words spoken to Lot's wife. Without a moment's thought she turned around and looked back. It was then that she was turned into a pillar of salt.

My God! For looking back she was turned into a pillar of salt? No it has nothing to do with the fact that Lot's wife looked back, it was the fact that she was not obedient to God's commandment. God gave her one commandment and that was to not look back and she, being human, turned and looked back.

In other words if you are not going to follow God's commandments what is the point of God keeping you on his earth?

Obedience is by far better than sacrifice. Without being obedient you will forfeit all of the peace and protection that has been promised to you. I said it once and I will repeat it a thousand times, I am not waiting until I die to get to heaven, I want some heaven here on earth.

Being obedient does not always feel good at the moment but always works for your good in the end. In fact the bible tells believers that all things work together for the good of those that love the Lord and were called upon his purpose.

Once you begin to trust God obedience in his commandments are sure to follow.

I know it's hard and God's word doesn't always make sense but he truly does know what's best for you. God told Lot's wife not to look back because he knew that the city was being destroyed and instead of her looking at what was behind her he wanted her to focus on what was ahead of her.

God has prepared an amazing future for you, but you mustn't look back. Be obedient and press forward for the crown of righteousness awaits you.

CHAPTER 21

LORD WHATEVER YOU ARE DOING, PLEASE DON'T DO IT WITHOUT ME

Everything that the Lord touches is good. When the Lord said let there be light, there was light. When the Lord said let the land produce living things according to their kind, it was so. When the Lord saw that man was lonely he made woman and it was good.

It appears that everything that the Lord does is good, so with that being said, anything that he does I pray that he includes me.

When you move without the Lord you are limited to what you can do and how far you are able to go. But when you move with the Lord you can go as high as the sky and farther than you have ever imagined.

We are a generation of people that seemingly like to take the short cuts in life. In other words we seem to be a "microwave" generation. We want it quick, fast, and in a hurry. But what you must understand is that what comes fast, will eventually leave even faster.

I have often noticed that when people are in need of help for work, ministry, and various other reasons they seem to call on their friends or "crew" for assistance. Now don't get me wrong I understand it is always easier to work with people whom you get along with, Lord knows everyday would be like heaven if I can pick and chose the people that work besides me on a daily basis. But the truth of the matter is that the only thing that will last is what God has ordained. Your "crew" will get tired and worn out before they truly get started because they were not placed there by God, instead you called them and they came running.

You have to learn how to slow down and seek God on all of your endeavors.

When you call man to work it will last for a season but when God calls you, you are given all that you need to endure for a lifetime.

I pray you seek God and that your prayer is whatever God does in this season; he includes you.

Heaven and earth shall pass away but the only thing that shall last is the word of God.

He is faithful and just to all who diligently seek him. Stop trying to do things in your own way; instead seek God and trust that he has your best intentions at heart not only during this season but in every season for the rest of your life.

CHAPTER 22

THAT OLD RUGGED CROSS

There is power at the cross. On the outside it looks like pieces of wood carved together. To the human eye it is nothing spectacular, nothing to awe about. But to those believers who knows what happened at the cross; it is more than just wood carved together.

See the cross is not where it ended but where it truly began. At that cross is where the most powerful love ever known to mankind begun.

The cross is where personal feelings were left behind and an unselfish act took place. That old rugged cross took the pain and hurt away and replaced it with peace and healing.

There is something about that cross that sets my soul on fire and makes my heart beat one thousand beats a minute.

Lord take me to the cross. Take me to the place where my sins were forgiven and I was redeemed. Take me to where the greatest love of all took place.

The older I get the more I appreciate my elders. I can appreciate the fact that they have now been through what I am now going through. The elders seem to have a sense of direction and integrity that is to be admired and the older they get, the wiser they seem to be.

Unfortunately they don't seem to get the respect that they deserve, some feel that elders are too old to remember or too old to understand, but if you would sit for a moment and allow them to reflect on what they have seen and what they know you would be surprised at what they can teach you.

Now please don't misinterpret what I am saying. In no way am I comparing the elders of today to an old rugged cross. What I want you to understand is that we have to learn how to appreciate the cross just as we do our elders.

The cross represents so much more that just the years that it has been rooted. It represents sacrifice and love. And though it may be tarnished it is still just as powerful today as it was 2000 years ago.

There is still power at the cross.

CHAPTER 23

WHAT SHALL I RENDER?

I don't posses riches and gold. Nor do I have a mansion on the top of a hill so what shall I render to a God who has full heartedly rendered everything for me?

The fact of the matter is that God does not want your earthly possession because he owns everything including the cattle in the fields. God only wants one thing; you. So what can you give the one who already has so much?

You can give him the one thing that money can't buy and the world doesn't poses; you can give him your heart and soul.

Giving God your heart and soul will not cost you a dime but may take a lifetime of commitment.

When you choose salvation you are choosing to freely give your soul to God. It doesn't matter what funeral arrangements your family makes or what final arrangement the church decides, because the fact of the matter is that God will already have your soul. When your soul is with God all is well because you are able to rest in his arms like a newborn baby dependant on a parent. Give God your soul today and won't have to worry about your tomorrow. Your whole life depends on that one very important decision. My soul firmly rests in the Lord.

If God has your soul not only is it simply beautiful, but it is truly amazing. When you can give him your heart as well as your soul you are truly in love and have learned what it means to trust God.

If you are anything like me your heart has been broken, betrayed, bruised, and hurt.

People who you thought were your friends turned out to be a foe. Those that you admired abused you, and even times when you thought your heart was healed someone somewhere has hurt you. You have two eyes, two ears, two hands, ten fingers, ten toes, two kidneys, yet one heart; one precious heart that beats twenty-four hours a day seven days a week, three-hundred sixty five days a year. One vital organ that is essential to your body. An organ that if it stops even for a second you may not live to see another day. You have trusted everyone with your heart, except the one who gave you his.

It is time that God has your heart. He yearns to be closer to you. He wants a relationship with all of his children and he deserves it.

Surrender your heart and soul to God. You tried everyone else and now it's time that you try Jesus.

CHAPTER 24

WHOSE HAND IS IT IN?

M y favorite professional athlete growing up was Michael Jordan. My dad and I would sit in front of the television from the start of the game until the very end. Though there were many talented players that played basketball, there was only one that I admired; Michael Jordan.

It seemed that every time his hand touched the basketball magic happened. Whether he shot a three-pointer or ran down the court and dunked, he was sure to please the crowd with his amazing basketball skills.

Yet amazingly when the ball was in the hand of other players it didn't seem to have the same affect as it did when Michael Jordan had it in his hands.

Which now poses me to ask the question whose hand is it in?

In my hand I can accomplish some things, but in the hand of God almighty I can do all things.

In your hand you can get a promotion on your job, but with God you can be the CEO of the company.

In my hand I can write and publish a few books, but in the hand of God I can become a best selling author.

So again I ask you, whose hand is it in?

Whose hand is your finance in, whose hand is the lives of your children in, whose hand is your emotions in, whose hand is in your tomorrows in?

I hope your life is in the hand of the almighty, all powerful, everlasting, great I am, alpha and omega. I hope your life is in the hand of God.

I put my life in my creators' hand and my life has never been the same. It seems that everything I touch turns to gold. Doors are now open that man can never close and I finally have the strength and willpower to make it to the finish line.

Put your life in the hand of the man who not only stilled the water but is capable of calming all seas. Put your hand in the hand of the man from Galilee.

CHAPTER 25

GOD KEPT ME

Police sirens and paramedics running in and out of the room, people screaming and crying, then the room door opens and someone stands over where I laid my head. The words that were spoken hurt me for years. Three simple words that made me think that I didn't stand a chance and I would never be able to get past that one night; "those poor children."

After that night my life has never been the same. That was the night that my mom left me but the Lord kept me.

As a young child I didn't know many things but one thing I still remember to this day is that God kept me when I was at my darkest hour. When people doubted me and friends were very few God wrapped his loving arms around me and assured me that he would never leave me nor would he forsake me.

It's been over twenty years since that night yet I still remember it as though it was yesterday. You see when you have an encounter with God your life is never the same. When you truly feel his touch there is no way that you can look at him the same. It's like the touch of a mother holding her new baby for the very first time. Though that mother doesn't know what the next eighteen years will bring her life is forever changed and she vows to sacrifice her life for her child.

God's love, like a true mothers' love, is unconditional. He keeps you in the midnight hour and when your money is funny, change is strange, family has left, and friends are few God is still there keeping you.

The bible assures us that though weeping may endure for a night joy will come in the morning light.

Wake up love, for morning is here.

CHAPTER 26

SEARCHED ALL OVER AND I FOUND NO ONE WHO COULD LOVE ME LIKE JESUS

I f only humans could love the way Jesus loves, what an amazing world this would be.

You will never understand what true genuine love is until you have fallen head over heels in love with Jesus. I know you think you have it all together and your relationship is for real but do you really understand the way Jesus loves you?

It was said more times than once that love is only felt in a sexual way and once you have felt that love with man there is no need to go searching for God.

Excuse me but you would have to be a fool to believe such an expression.

Man's love feels good for a few hours (if you are lucky) but God's love feels good for a lifetime.

In other words with God's love you are able to reach your climax from the time you awake until the time he puts you back to sleep each night not wanting for anything seven days a week three hundred sixty five days a year.

God has a way of loving you down to your soul. He purposely places his spirit inside of you so that when you are lonely he can give you comfort, when you are weak he can strengthen you, when you are tired he can carry you along the way.

You may have searched all over, from the city to the fields but if you have searched and still can't find the kind of love that I speak about it may be because you are searching in the wrong place.

You see the God that I serve is omnipresent, in other words he is at the same place at the same time. There is no need to look for him for he has already been found standing in front of you. His arms are stretched wide open willing and ready to hold the way you need to be held.

He is everything that you need and more, from that lawyer in the courtroom, to that best friend you need to talk with late at night, he is God and God all by himself.

Stop searching for him because I promise you he has already found you. In fact the bible tells us that God knew us before we were even born and has already set us apart.

There is no greater love than the love of God. Don't take my word for it; try him for yourself.

CHAPTER 27

I VOW TO PRAISE YOU LORD

It is pay-day; we have paid all of our bills and still have money left over to have fun on the weekend. We are now happy and we insist on praising the name of the Lord; in fact we will sing every gospel song we know and love at the top of our lungs.

But let hell break loose. Let us have one bill overdue or a child acting out, and we complain instead of pray, cry instead of shout praises, and argue instead of wait for an answered prayer.

Lord help us all.

We should not just give conditional praises. A conditional praise is when someone can praise God only during certain conditions. Some that conditionally praise only praise God only when things are going well, while others only praise God when things are going wrong.

We must all transition from giving conditional praises and willingly become unconditional worshippers who can praise God through any and every situation.

It is nearly impossible to change overnight. In fact if you try and change too fast you may miss the most important part of the growing process. A child doesn't go from the fifth grade straight to the eleventh grade. Instead they slowly make the transition one grade level at a time. They take it one school year at a time and they are taught everything that they need in order to effectively make it through to the next grade level.

Just as a child transitions in school we too as adults have to go through different transitional stages in our lives. If you ever want to transition from being someone who praises God conditionally to someone who praises unconditional it is time that you make a vow to allow God to work on you so that you may be able to praise God at all times.

CHAPTER 28

IF GOD NEVER BLESSES ME AGAIN; HE HAS ALREADY DONE ENOUGH

I f I don't live to see my family grow older, or if I don't get to travel this great country I would still be okay. If I don't live to see the next president of the United States, or wake up to see tomorrow, it is okay because God has already done enough.

God has truly been better to me than I have been to myself. He has provided for me and kept me and continued to love me through all of my pain. God has done more for me than I can comprehend and he has truly in one way or another done enough for you.

My prayer is for one day, only twenty four hours this world would not ask God for anything but simple thank God for everything. For he is a good God and he is so very worthy to be praised.

My soul gets happy just thinking about his marvelous works and wonders.

The bible says that everything that has breath ought to praise the Lord.

I don't know about you but I vow to give honor where honor is due.

God is a good God. He is sovereign and just. God blesses me more than man ever could and more than this old world should.

Learn how to bless the name of the Lord.

Give him the glory that he is worthy of receiving. Stop always asking and learn how to be thankful.

Thank God as often as you possibly can. Do you not know that when the blessings go up the praises come down?

I will bless the Lord at all times, for if he never blesses be again, he has already done enough.

CHAPTER 29

THERE IS A STORY BEHIND MY PRAISE

I said it once and I will say it again, until you know my story you will never understand my glory.

Others may never understand why you praise God the way you do or why you rush into the house of the Lord as much as you do. But only you know what God has brought you through and what he is capable in during in your life.

God has been good to me. He has taken me in when all others has counted me out. He has dried my eyes in the mid-night hour and turned all of my darkness into marvelous days. God has talked to me through suicidal thoughts and assured me that my tomorrows would be better than my today.

There is a story behind my praise, and you may not understand it, that's fine because it isn't for you. I praise God because he is my only source of strength; he is my protector, my shield in time of trouble. My praise is for real and there is a story behind my praise.

Now maybe you don't have a story yet, bless your heart. But if you keep on living you will understand what I am talking about. You will understand why it's more than just a Sunday morning shout or Wednesday night worship; it's a lifestyle.

Learn how to praise God on purpose. Learn how to lift him up on the good days and pray even harder during the bad days.

When you do you will be able to appreciate who God is and allow him to work in your life in the way that he sees fit. Let me repeat that, I said you will be able to allow God to work in your life in the way that he (God) sees fit.

Stop trying to be a superhero. Let go and let God. And when you do you will learn how to praise God on purpose just for whom he is and what he has done in your life thus far.

CHAPTER 30

MY PAIN HAS BEEN TURNED INTO PRAISE

Job was a just man in the sight of the Lord. He lived a life pleasing and acceptable. He seemed to have it all together. He was married, had children, owned houses, and cattle; he seemed to be living the perfect life. But all that changed the night that God allowed Satan to come into Job's life. Job lost his children, his wife wanted him to curse the name of the Lord, his cattle died, and fires raged through homes.

It seemed like life for Job was over. But Job was not just anybody. He wasn't a convenient Christian, you know the ones that call on God on Sunday and cause hell on Monday.

Job was a righteous man, in fact even after losing so much Job still blessed the name of the Lord as he understood that just like he came naked into this world it is the same way that he shall leave.

Job understood that his pain was temporary because his life on earth was but for a moment. He knew that God would be waiting for him on the other side and the pain he felt at that moment would be turned into true genuine praise in the end.

According to the bible after heartache and pain Job was blessed with double than what he had before. Let me say that again; the bible says that Job was blessed with double than what he had before.

Somebody ought to take a praise break and shout!!

Just as God turned Job's pain into praise he is more than able to do the same for you and me.

We all seem to want heaven but we aren't willing to go through some hell.

In your life you will have some mountains in front of you, but the bible says that with faith we can move those mountains. In other words I don't have to waste time climbing to the other side, if I just increase my faith in God I can speak and that mountain, by faith, shall move.

Are you in pain? Give that pain to God. Let him turn your pain into praise.

It will by far be the best thing you have ever done in your life.

My pain has been turned into praise. If God did it for me, he can surely do it for you.

CHAPTER 31

MY WORSHIP IS FOR REAL

In the book of Revelations it says that every living thing worshipped the Lord for twenty four hours. They obviously understood what true worship was.

When you worship God for real nothing else matters during that worship time but God, and the glorification of his great name.

Anyone can sing a song of praise or say a morning prayer but when you truly begin to worship God it becomes more than worship; it becomes a lifestyle.

Real worship doesn't just happen on Sunday morning it happens on Monday evening, Tuesday at work, Wednesday night bible study, Thursday during noon day, Friday at home and Saturday with the family. Worship happens anytime God's presence is being sought and can be felt by one of his children.

How does your worship become for real? I am so glad you asked. Worship is real when your heart is in it. When your soul begins to cry out to the Lord it is then that you begin to receive him in a way that is like no other.

When you begin to worship for real you are able to go higher with God because you begin to reverence him and seek his face. The bible says in James that the closer you grow to God, the closer God will draw to you. Don't you want that closeness to your loving father? I know I do so instead of waiting until Sunday morning I vow to worship him everyday.

I worship him because he has been a good God. I worship him because he is holy. I worship him because he has never left my side. I worship him because he talks with me and walks with me. I worship him because he is just. I worship him because he saw the best in me when everyone else saw the worst in me. I worship him because he saw fit for me to live one more day. I worship him because he is able to do anything but fell. I worship him because he is by far the best thing that has ever happened to me.

My worship is for real. Let your worship be for real. Seek God for yourself, call upon his name and give yourself away to him.

CHAPTER 32

I SHALL HAVE THE DESIRES OF MY HEART

In 2009 when I fully submitted myself to God I excitedly made a list of seven things that I wanted from God. The list included a closer relationship with God, good paying career, husband, children, new car, house, and to be healthy. I just knew that once I had all seven of the requests on my list that I would then be able to experience full happiness and joy. I would sit back, relax, and think about how happy receiving all of the desires of my heart would make me.

Of all the things I received was the one that I had first on my list; a closer walk with God. I received it and I transitioned from my old self into a new creature in Christ. It was during my transition that I began to realize that I have all that I need as long as I have God and with God I have all of the desires of my hearts.

When you have God, you have enough. He shall supply all of your needs according to his riches. In other words God will give you what you need when you need it in the manner in which he sees fit.

That doesn't mean you can petition God for a new car today and receive it tomorrow. It isn't the name it and claim it game. God doesn't work on your timetable. He works in his own timing and in his own matter.

The key to remember is that God always has your best intentions in mind. His intend is never to hurt you or hinder your walk. In fact it is the exact opposite.

God intends to break you down from what you were and build you up to what he intends for you to be. In other words he is the potter and you are the clay. He patiently takes you apart piece by piece than in his own special way he builds you back up. But he doesn't build you up in a way that you think you should be, instead he shows you the plans he has for your life and builds you in a way that you can handle all that he has purposely planned for you. Your ways are not of God's. You will never truly understand the mystery of God or the ways of all the miraculous wonders he performs.

The bible says that he will give you the desires of your heart when you delight yourself in him. What God will do is change your desire to his will for your life. Take my advice and let God mold you. Let him shape you and break you so that when he does build you back up you will be tougher that before and you will be built to last through any trials and tribulation, heartbreak or pain.

I shall have the desires of my heart, by any means necessary in Jesus name.

CHAPTER 33

LORD SHOW ME THE ERROR OF MY WAYS

I have messed up more times than I can count. I have made the wrong decisions and purposely went the wrong way. I have been disobedient because of the lack of trust and missed out on blessings. But on this day at this moment, I ask that the Lord would show me the errors of my ways.

All have fallen short of the glory of the Lord. It doesn't matter who you are or how long you have been doing your best to live right, you have fallen short.

Right now my prayer is that God will gracefully show you the error of your ways. I pray that where you lack forgiveness he opens your heart and where you are disobedient he shows you how to obey his commands.

Without God showing you your errors you, like the Israelites will wander in circle. You will not be able to reach your highest potential until you have been washed and purged of all wrong in your life.

Sin is what separates you from your savior. Though God hates the sin he loves the sinner.

Ask God to show you the errors of your ways. Seek God for yourself. Call on his name. The bible says that he will answer all that diligently seek him. Seek him in the morning and seek him late at night. Seek him now while he may be found. Seek him because he is the only one that is able to keep you from falling.

Lord I pray that you will show each of your children the errors of their ways. Don't let them make the same mistake again on today. Let them be able to walk boldly in your sight. Keep them as they travel from day to day. Allow them to be right in your sight, in Jesus name amen.

CHAPTER 34

IT'S NOT A RELIGION;
IT'S A RELATIONSHIP

Catholic, Baptist, Jehovah witness, Pentecostal, and Mormons are all respected religions but at the end of the day when it's all said and done religions do not get you to heaven. The truth of the matter is that it is not about religion but about a relationship.

While attending a funeral there was some controversy over the fact that the deceased person did not have the appropriate religious attire on inside of the casket. The argument became so heated that one of the clergies in charge stormed out of the respected worship center. Now I am no one to judge nor do I assume to know all there is to know about religion, but one thing that I do know is that if the deceased is not already sleeping with the Lord, religious attire will not get the person to heaven.

The religious attire was part of tradition. Tradition is what can hold religious people back. Tradition is what your grandmother used to do and now as a result your mother does it and now you do it. It gets past down sometimes "just because". We have to slowly break from tradition and seek God's direction. The bible says seek and you shall find. It is time to seek God and patiently wait for the direction that he gives us. You must then be receptive to what God tells you. He is real and yearns for a relationship with all of his children. In fact just like a Sheppard goes after one lost sheep so does your father in heaven go after his child that is lost and in need of a fathers' love and guidance.

When we die our souls will go on to be with the Lord. Our body, clothes, and all of our earthly possessions will remain on earth.

We have to get it through our heads that it is not about religion but it is about a personal relationship. We sometimes get so caught up with religion that we forget what matters the most; a relationship.

A relationship is what connects us to one another and helps keep us committed.

Just as you seek a relationship with your spouse, children, and family members you should seek a relationship with the Lord. Don't settle for just a religion, it's time to commit to a full fledge relationship.

The process may take longer than expected, but it will be well worth the transition.

CHAPTER 35

WHEN JESUS DIED HE HAD ME IN MIND

Why in the world would anyone in their right mind sacrifice their entire life for a perfect stranger?

Some of us barely stop to give the man standing on the corner a few dollars let alone even think of sacrificing our lives for them?

So why would Jesus willingly die? He died for me, he died for you. Jesus died for the young boy who wants to grown up to become a fire fighter and the teenage girl who dreams of one day seeing her name in lights. He died for that man who vowed to be the best dad to his children and the woman who is expecting to one day when an Oscar award.

What actually went through the mind of Jesus the day he breathed his last breath you and I may never know. How he felt that long dark day remains a mystery to this day. But one thing I do know that is very clear is that he died for you and me.

The death of Jesus is truly the ultimate sacrifice. That is an example of uncompromising love, a love that was so pure and prefect, a love that can not be measured nor can ever be duplicated.

When Jesus hung his head low he was committing himself not to his death, but for you to be able to live your life.

Don't let his death be in vein. Don't let the blood, sweat, and tears of our savior be for nothing. If you can't think of one reason why you personally want to honor the life of Jesus and live accordingly then let me take a moment and explain to you why it is important that you do not take his death lightly.

It is Jesus' death that not only represents sacrifice but it shows love. Love is so powerful that if done in the right manner and expressed at the right time, it can put you on cloud nine and you will not ever have to come down. Love is what keeps up connected. It is because of love that we are free, because of love that we can smile when we want to cry, and laugh at our past mistakes only to make better future choices.

Love is saying not my will father, but yours. Love is about sacrificing and learning to let go and trust. Love is what keeps a family together and brings departed children back home to parents.

Love is being beaten and assaulted though you have done nothing wrong believing and having faith that it is all part of God's plan.

Love is staying in a borrowed tomb until the exact day and hour your father tells you that it is the appointed time to get up.

Love is never complaining.

Love is spending forty days and forty nights in the desert though you are getting tempted by the enemy.

Love is being bold enough to trust your father even when everyone has turned against you.

Love is walking the earth waiting patiently for people to change.

Love is being the same yesterday, today, and forever more just so that people will see that you are consistent.

Love is dying for sinners to be saved.

Love is what your father did when he sent his only begotten son to walk the earth and go to preach a revival in hell just so you can one day make it into heaven.

Uncompromising love is making the ultimate sacrifice because you have all of God's children in mind.

When Jesus died he did it for you and he did it for me.

Don't let that sacrificial death be in vein.